30 Days
To Stop Being An
Asshole

A Mindfulness Program with a Touch of Humor

Harper Daniels

Copyright © JV 2021

Share your journey!

Let people know you're practicing mindfulness! Post a picture of the cover and include #30DaysNow via social media. Our various guides share the same lessons, so you can see how others are using mindfulness on their journey!

Don't forget that each exercise has a unique hashtag for online sharing.

A WHIMSICAL APPROACH TO MINDFULNESS AND MEDITATION

This book is meant to be a guide only, and does not guarantee specific results. If the lessons and exercises in this book are followed, change can occur for certain people. Results vary from person to person; some people may not need to complete the thirty days to experience change, but it's encouraged that the entire program be read completely through at least once.

The last half of the book consists of blank note pages that the reader can use in conjunction with the exercises for each day. The reader is encouraged to utilize the note pages; though it's not necessary.

Give the gift of mindfulness. See similar guides at www.30DaysNow.com if you wish to purchase a book for a loved one. **See the disclosure below.**

Disclosure (Shared Lessons and Exercises):
Keep in mind that our mindfulness guides share the same lessons and exercises, so there is no need to purchase more than one book; unless you are sharing with a group or giving the guides as gifts. Our mindfulness guides are created for various topics; however, they utilize the same lessons and exercises, so please be aware of this before purchasing. For example, *30 Days to Stop Being an Asshole* will mostly have the same lessons and exercises as *30 Days to Reduce Stress* and so forth. By reading just one of our guides, you'll be able to apply the same lessons and exercises to multiple areas of your life.

Enjoy your journey of self-discovery!

Contents

Preface..4

Day 1...8
Day 2...9
Day 3...10
Day 4...11
Day 5...12
Day 6...13
Day 7...14
Day 8...15
Day 9...16
Day 10...17
Day 11...18
Day 12...19
Day 13...20
Day 14...21
Day 15...22
Day 16...23
Day 17...24
Day 18...25
Day 19...26
Day 20...27
Day 21...28
Day 22...29
Day 23...30
Day 24...31
Day 25...32
Day 26...33
Day 27...34
Day 28...35
Day 29...36
Day 30...37

Conclusion..38
Note Pages..............................Begins on 39

Preface

Has someone said to you, "*You're an asshole!*" Maybe a few people have said this to you; or maybe you have enough understanding to realize that you are one. How can you even know if you are an authentic, callous, heartless, bitter, and cruel asshole? This 30 day mindfulness program will help you to stop being an asshole; but let's first define *asshole* for the purpose of this book.

Asshole has become a broad term used in western civilization to describe people, primarily males, who are excessively inconsiderate, selfish, arrogant, rude, and disrespectful. The female equivalent to an asshole is typically referred to as a *bitch*. It's important that you realize that the word asshole has an expansive definition, like *bitch*, and is often used as a general insult; however, let's say that the five adjectives just mentioned define the word fairly well.

To make it even easier to understand, let's just say that an asshole is a person, usually male, with a habit of being regularly disrespectful, arrogant, and inconsiderate. If you're following this program, you probably have a keen realization that you may be an asshole, or exhibit asshole tendencies. If so, don't worry, because this 30 day mindfulness program will help you; and more importantly, will guide you away from the pernicious habits, feelings, and patterns of thinking that keep you trapped as a bona fide asshole.

It's critical that you not participate in this guided program for someone else; such as a significant other that might have said, "*I want you to read '30 Days to Stop Being an Asshole'...or we're done with this relationship,*" or, "*You're such as asshole. Read this and you'll see I'm *right!*" If anyone has marketed this book to you in that fashion, then that person is being an asshole, or bitch. To get the most out of this program, you must participate in these exercises and lessons for yourself.

It might be that you're not a chronic asshole; it could be that you're concerned about adopting thought patterns and habits that can change you into one. Thankfully, this program can be applied to many different dependencies, habits, and unhealthy ways of thinking; so you'll benefit from the program regardless of being a problematic asshole or not. If intuition is telling you that you might have an asshole seed growing - planted after a bad breakup, failure, disappointment, lifestyle change, loss of money, loss of job, onslaught of insults, etc – then this book will be an immense help, to prevent that seed from growing into an oak tree-sized issue that totally ruins your life.

The following pages involve a 30 day mindfulness program made up of lessons and exercises to help you stop being an asshole. Though these lessons and exercises can be applied to any adverse thought patterns and behaviors, this program will focus specifically on asshole tendencies and ways of thinking.

For some readers, their unhealthy perceptions and behaviors will drop quickly; and for others, the drop will happen gradually. In either case, if you stick with the program you'll start to witness your cruelties diminish and you'll eventually stop being an asshole. Don't critique your progress throughout the program, as this isn't a competition and there isn't a goal you must attain. Let the asshole dependency drop as you work through the exercises and lessons.

It's not necessary to complete these days in order, nor should you be religious about completing them successfully. There is no such thing as a successful completion of this program. The bottom line is to observe and awaken, and that cannot be obtained through success, force, pressure, struggle, or competition. Simply relax, follow the program, and you'll enjoy a new and wonderful state of being, without being an asshole.

You'll also notice that mindfulness, silence, and stillness are a regular discipline for each day. Because you've been influenced by a society that demands instant gratification, silence and stillness may seem nearly impossible for you to practice. For this reason, we'll incorporate this discipline from the outset. A quiet and still mind is an incredibly powerful resource, but one that requires daily maintenance.

It should also be noted that you're not required to stop being an asshole during this program. However, if you have already gone a few days without being an asshole, then it's advised that you continue that momentum; but as mentioned, don't make it a struggle. The point being: by practicing the following disciplines in the days to come, you won't even need willpower to stop being an asshole; you'll sense asshole thoughts and temptations coming and going, but they won't have the slightest impact. Simply put, you'll drop all desire to continue being an asshole.

One of the most important lessons to keep in mind is to not fight asshole tendencies or strive against them while participating in these exercises. If you find yourself being an asshole during the coming days, then that's completely fine as long as you stick to the program. Remember, be careful not to develop a spirit of fighting or competition during this program – dependencies and habits thrive on conflict.

You'll need about 15-30 minutes per day for the program; but feel free to spend more time if needed. The amount of time doesn't matter, as long as you're in an environment that allows you to concentrate without distraction. Also to be mentioned, the last portion of this book includes note pages that you can use with the exercises. It's encouraged that you write down any thoughts, insights, adaptations, lessons, mantras, etc…on those blank pages. The note pages can also be used to rip out and take with you. Feel free to use them as you wish.

One last thing: If you're like most people in the modern world, you might be dependent on caffeine, alcohol, or sugar to some extent. If you are, do your best to lessen the consumption of these substances over the next 30 days. Can you cut consumption of these substances in half, or more? It's important that your mind is sober and your body relaxed to get the most out of these exercises and stop being an asshole.

Let's get started.

Let others know you're practicing mindfulness! Post a picture of the cover and include #30DaysNow. Also, don't forget that each exercise has a unique hashtag for online sharing.

Share your journey and discover other people practicing mindfulness!

Day 1
(Share this experience using #30DaysBreathing)

Exercise:

Find a place without distraction, and turn off all electronics. Sit with your back straight, kneel, or lie on a hard surface (not bed) and remain in silence for 10 minutes.

During these 10 minutes, take deep and focused breaths and hold them for a few seconds each. Exhale slowly. Listen intently to your breathing. Don't try to change it – simply listen, and feel the air go in and out.

When you're ready, repeat the mantra: **"Be still. Be silent."** *Repeat this slowly multiple times out loud as well as quietly. You might experience boredom or anxiety, but continue repeating the mantra regardless. Repeat it until you're calm and focused. You can continue the deep breathing during the mantra, or take deep breaths during pauses. Don't rush.*

Each of the 30 days will have this time of silence, focused breathing, and a mantra. Except for this page, the end of each day will remind you of the minutes you are to spend in silence and focused breathing; and will also have a mantra for you to practice. You can repeat the mantras during your times of silence and focused breathing, or following. Remember, there is no right or wrong way to do this.

Adverse dependencies want to fight; in fact, they're energized by fighting. Instead of fighting an inner asshole, meet it with silence and observation. Let the exercises and lessons in this program guide you.

Day 2
(Share this experience using #30DaysPonder)

Exercise:

Ponder this question: Can you remember a time in your life when you weren't an asshole?

Writing is extremely beneficial to the mind; especially when pondering. Write down your thoughts about this particular question. If your mind drifts, then write whatever thoughts emerge. It's okay if you have nothing to write, but ponder the question regardless.

Were you able to remember a period in your life when you weren't exhibiting asshole behavior? If you're like many people in western civilization, you may have to return to memories of childhood to determine that period. It's not uncommon for a person to learn to become an asshole at an early age. Assholes have often been influenced, motivated, and taught by other assholes within society.

Recognize that being an asshole is a learned behavior with roots. However, it can be dropped quickly and completely; and you have the capability to drop it.

*10 minutes of silence and focused breathing. Repeat the mantra: *"**Drop. Unlearn. Discover.**"*

Day 3

(Share this experience using #30DaysIdentity)

Exercise:

On a piece of paper, write down all the labels and adjectives that you and others use to identify you.

For example, do you see yourself as a son, daughter, mother, father, student, teacher, cashier, friend, engineer, accountant, employee, employer, roommate, husband, wife, etc? And what adjectives do you use to label yourself; for example, do you identify yourself as failed, successful, happy, depressed, good, moral, unethical, lustful, greedy, valuable, worthless, etc? Don't only write down the labels and descriptions you perceive; but also write down what you believe others label you as: do you believe others see you as a valuable friend, stupid and incompetent employee, extremely smart and talented worker, etc? Take as long as you need, and fill up a sheet of paper with those labels and descriptions.

After you've done that, tear the paper into multiple pieces and throw it away. Those labels and adjectives mean nothing. They're not "you." You cannot be defined, labeled, described, or controlled by titles. Most people poison their conscience with such learned vocabulary. They really believe these words hold power – they'll even fight, stress out, become ill, and die to make these words part of reality. Asshole behavior dependency, as well as most societal tools, teaches you to identify with particular words, which are only thoughts. Unlearn them.

*10 minutes of silence and focused breathing. Repeat the mantra: "**I am not a label, title, or description.**"

Day 4
(Share this experience using #30DaysPatience)

Exercise:

Listen to a person intently without interruption. Only speak if the person asks you a question, but don't give a long answer. Make the conversation entirely theirs. Give them the floor, and listen to every word they are saying. Again, do not interrupt. Observe their words and facial expressions without judgment. Be patient and relaxed, even if they speak for more than a few minutes.

Patience is a dying practice in our digital age. It appears that all business involves the perceived need to go faster, faster, and faster. Quicker responses, faster uploads, more data, rapid analysis, accelerated transportation, and all sorts of chop-chop. This false need for speed has seeped deep into our collective psyche. The western world is filled with anxiously demanding people, going nowhere fast.

This widespread lack of patience has caused a problem with regard to listening to one another. It has also caused dependency on asshole ways of thinking and behaving to manifest extensively. Practicing patience by listening intently to someone speak is a great way to slow down the mind and build meaningful relationships. The hypnotic feelings of being an asshole cannot compete with real human interaction, which requires patience.

*10 minutes of silence and focused breathing. Repeat the mantra: **"Listen. Be patient. Listen."**

Day 5
(Share this experience using #30DaysBlue)

Exercise:

Today, look for the color blue in your surrounding environment. If possible, spend the entire day looking for the color blue in the places you go. Whether you're doing this exercise in a bedroom, office, classroom, outside, or while traveling, look for the color blue in all things that surround you. If you think you'll forget to do this throughout the entire day, spend at least 20 focused minutes practicing this exercise at some point.

Focused attention is something that must be practiced - it doesn't come easy in our rapid paced society. Instead of encouraging us to focus and observe, the modern world encourages us to rush and get things done.

Searching for a color or shape helps to slow down our accelerated and cyclical thought patterns, and reminds us that there's more to the world than the chaotic thoughts we collectively and daily experience. By searching for the color blue, your mind can escape the fictitious grip of anxiety, lust, desire, depression, worry, fear, or any other potent emotion. When you are experiencing asshole thoughts and behaviors, are you aware of the colors around you? Most likely not.

Asshole patterns of thinking function to distract and remove your conscience from present reality. Look for the color blue today, and wake up to life in the present moment.

*10 minutes of silence and focused breathing. Repeat the mantra: "*I am focused, here and now.*"*

Day 6

(Share this experience using #30DaysBody)

Exercise:

Observe your body. Observe how it feels, moves, and reacts. More direction is explained below.

If you're still caught in an asshole mode, observe your body movements, sounds, sensations, and breaths while being an asshole. Do your eyes look down or roll? Do you move your hands fast or slow? Does your voice rise or lower? How is your posture? Do you smile or frown? Try to observe everything about your body while being an asshole. Be aware of its affect on your body.

If you are not being an asshole today, then continue with the 10 minutes of silence and focused breathing, but get in touch with your body. A good way to do this is by touching each body part and saying its name, leaving your hand on the part for a few seconds and feeling its texture and warmth. Start with your head: place your hand on your head and say, "*I am touching my head.*" And then work your way down to your shoulders, arms, stomach, legs, knees, and feet. Focus your attention on one body part at a time. Say its name and describe what you are touching.

*10 minutes of silence and focused breathing. Repeat the mantra: "*I am not my body.*"

Day 7

(Share this experience using #30DaysGSR)

Exercise:

Say the words "Guilt", "Shame", and "Regret" 10 times to yourself out loud. Don't rush. Pause between each repetition. For the pause, you can take a deep breath. Your eyes can remain open or closed. Again, don't rush - say the words slowly and observe any thoughts, feelings, or images that emerge internally.

Now, say these words again 10 times, but with a smile.

What futile credence we give words such as Guilt, Shame and Regret. We use these words on ourselves as well as others; they become regular vocabulary for our internal recurring voices. And in the end, they're mere words that hold no power. What would these words be without a facial expression, tone, inflection, or emphasis?

When you said these three specific words, what thoughts came to mind, what did you feel, and was there a reaction in your body? If there is a reaction, such as shortness of breath or a frown, people tend to interpret it as sadness; but this reaction is a learned behavior. We've been taught to feel and think a certain way with regard to guilt, shame, and regret. The truth is: these words mean nothing.

Asshole behavior, like most dependencies, flourishes on these three words and the learned reactions they produce. But see them for what they are...mere words with no power.

*10 minutes of silence and focused breathing. Repeat the mantra: *"I am not Guilt, Shame, or Regret."*

Day 8
(Share this experience using #30DaysPhone)

Exercise:

Turn off your cell phone, or put it in airplane mode, for at least 1 hour, and observe the thoughts you experience. If you don't have any major responsibilities this day, or if you have all you need and don't require the phone, then turn off your cell phone for 12 hours. This exercise works best if you can go 24 hours without your cell phone activated; but go no less than 1 hour. If there are people who are immediately dependent on you, send them a text saying that you'll be unavailable, and then turn off your phone.

Like never before in history, we live in a modern world with a plethora of distractions. These distractions fight for our attention, because money is behind the scenes. Every business is wondering how they can break your distraction from one thing so that you can be distracted by their thing. It's a constant war between everyone; and the businesses that can influence the most assholes, wins. Whoever can hold your attention the longest, wins the battle; but whoever can make you dependent, wins the war. The smartphone has become a primary channel for these businesses to influence asshole behavior.

Asshole dependent companies need for you to be distracted by their business; otherwise you might wake up to reality and enjoy the beauty of life, which includes living happily in the present moment. Asshole behavior has made its way into smartphones, and companies want you to become the most dependent asshole out there; so power off your phone.

*10 minutes of silence and focused breathing. Repeat the mantra: "**I am not distracted. I am here and now.**"

Day 9

(Share this experience using #30DaysGuess)

Exercise:

What will your next thought be?

Try to guess what your next thought, or next two thoughts, will be.

Five minutes from now; will you be thinking about love, work, family, a burrito, tomorrow, money, etc? We're not in control of our thoughts, and that scares people. We may be able to influence our thought patterns, but thoughts are more or less like clouds that come and go in a big blue sky. It's difficult to predict what clouds will be floating through our minds this week, let alone in five minutes.

By asking the question, *"What will my next thought be?"* you're allowing yourself to escape a thought cluttered mind for a few moments and experience thoughtlessness – which is fresh, wonderful, new, and present.

After you've attempted to answer that question, observe what thoughts actually do float into your mind. Observe them like you would clouds in the sky. You'll realize that you're not your thoughts, which are often fantasy and not based in the present moment.

The goal of asshole behavior is to send you an endless amount of fictitious thoughts; so many that you actually believe they're part of your being. Thoughts are not real.

*10 minutes of silence and focused breathing. Repeat the mantra: *"I am not the thoughts I experience. They will pass."*

Day 10
(Share this experience using #30DaysTrash)

Exercise:

Go out and buy a small trash can. You should be able to find one cheaply. If you don't have the funds for this exercise, you can use an empty box or container; however, a small trash can works better for its symbolism.

Designate this specific trash can your "concerns and worries can" (or use any title you wish) – some people benefit from writing this label directly onto the can.

Now, write down (on scraps of paper or whatever paper you wish to use) any concerns, worries, and adverse thoughts that you may be experiencing today, and throw them into the can. Try to practice this every day: quickly write down worries, concerns, and negative thoughts, and then throw them into the can. It may be beneficial to have a supply of scrap paper near the can for easy access.

This exercise may seem simple, but let's go beyond throwing your written concerns, worries, and thoughts away. Designate a few times during the week for sifting through the can and taking out random worries and concerns from days prior – just reach in and pull some out. Observe them, but don't judge yourself. This is a great exercise to learn your negative thought patterns and the lies that grip your conscience. If you stick with this practice, you may gain a deeper understanding into the dependencies, habits, thought patterns, and feelings that have you stuck as an asshole.

*10 minutes of silence and focused breathing. Repeat the mantra: "**There is nothing to worry about. All is well.**"

Day 11

(Share this experience using #30DaysLetter)

Exercise:

Write a letter or email to yourself. There is something about using pen and paper that is very effective when writing letters, but feel free to write an email if you wish. Don't send the letter or email, just write it and save it for a day – you can toss it out or delete it tomorrow.

Write anything that comes to mind: It can be advice you want to give yourself, a story from the past, random thoughts and feelings, frustrations and worries, things you're thankful for, etc. There is no right or wrong – write whatever comes to mind in the moment. Try to write at least two full paragraphs.

What was the theme and voice of your message? Was it a positive or negative tone? Were you advising yourself? Did you make any judgments about yourself? Did you start demanding that you should or should not do something? Was the letter full of gratitude? Was there anger and despair? Read the letter as if you were reading it from a friend – is it a letter that would upset you, or one that you would welcome with excitement and a smile?

Whatever you wrote is essentially being written on the tablet of your mind. This exercise is useful for getting to know the internal voice that we all have in our minds. It's an internal voice that can change for the better with observation, acceptance, and awareness. Be aware of your internal voice in the present moment.

*10 minutes of silence and focused breathing. Repeat the mantra: "*I am not my internal voice. I am aware.*"*

Day 12
(Share this experience using #30DaysLose)

Exercise:

Choose an object that you use and rely on every day, and that you sometimes lose – such as a key, cell phone, pen, hat, toothbrush, or television controller.

Now, actually attempt to lose this object. Hide it well, and try to make yourself forget where it is.

More than likely you won't be able to lose this object, as hard as you try, because you have applied a lot of attention to the process of losing it and trying to make yourself forget. At this point, losing it is nearly impossible. Why do you think this is?

If you try to drop a dependency, behavior, thought pattern, addiction, or any unhealthy vice using a lot of thought, attention, focus, struggle, and effort...you'll never lose it. It will be with you in one form or another for a very long time, possibly forever. The point is: whatever you give attention to consistently, will be difficult to lose. This is the reason why people who complain a lot are never happy – they can't stop giving thought and attention to the problems they're grumbling about. The problems eventually become an intimate part of their lives. Remember, rival enemies maintain a devoted relationship.

Don't fight asshole behavior and patterns of thinking; instead, come into the present moment. Happiness is now.

*10 minutes of silence and focused breathing. Repeat the mantra: **"I do not need to hold on. I allow it to be lost."**

Day 13

(Share this experience using #30DaysScribble)

Exercise:

Take a piece of paper (any size, but large enough to draw on); with a pen, scribble a random line with your eyes closed. Don't lift your pen from the paper; keep it as one messy scribble. Only spend two or three seconds doing this.

Now, with your eyes open and seeing what your scribble looks like, make it into an actual image of something. Work with the scribble to make something noticeable.

What did you make out of your scribble: an animal, house, drifting balloon, kite, a person, a scenario, an entire scene with many things, etc?

This is one of my favorite exercises. It's a lesson that teaches that the scribbles and confusions we experience in life can be changed and formed with a new perspective. Life is all about perspective. How do you perceive scribble, mess, chaos, clutter, disarray, and confusion in your life experience? Do you know that you can perceive it differently starting now?

In silence, stillness, and with an open mind, take a look at any scribbles that you may be experiencing in life. If you observe long enough, without judgment or concern, you will gain a new perspective.

*10 minutes of silence and focused breathing. Repeat the mantra: ***I am not confused. My perception can always change in the present moment.***"

Day 14
(Share this experience using #30DaysBathroom)

Exercise:

This exercise may seem frivolous, but give it a try; because it may be one of the lessons that benefit you most.

For the remainder of the day, whenever you use the bathroom, for any reason, take your time with what you're doing. Don't rush through the process, like you may normally do. Focus on taking your time in the bathroom; do every step of your bathroom experience twice as slow. It may even help to say each step: "I am now sitting up straight on the toilet," "I am now putting soap on my hands," "I am now drying my hands," etc.

Most people hurry up their bathroom experience, not realizing what they're doing – forcing, not standing or sitting straight, not relaxing, not washing their hands properly, not drying their hands slowly. They rush in and out, like they have somewhere important to go. Don't be like that any longer. Take your time in the bathroom; it's not only unhealthy for the body to rush the excretion process, but it's also unhealthy for the mind. A rushed bathroom experience doesn't allow you to live in the present moment. Allow the excretion and cleaning to happen naturally with relaxed and focused attention.

The patterns of thinking as an asshole require rushing, worrying, and hurrying. Slow down considerably, and the asshole dependency will drop.

*10 minutes of silence and focused breathing. Repeat the mantra: **"Don't hurry. Stay present. Stay still."**

Day 15
(Share this experience using #30DaysPassing)

Exercise:

On a piece of paper (any size) write down the name of your current emotion. For example, at this moment you might be feeling agitated, calm, bored, angry, anxious, excited, etc. Whatever emotion you are experiencing, give it a name and put it on paper.

Now, write down "I'm experiencing this emotion in the present moment and it will pass. It's only an emotion."

You can throw the paper away, or hold onto it if you wish.

Similar to how we give certain words credence, we tend to give our emotions a lot of trust. We also tend to blame the outside world for emotions we are feeling: *"They made me angry," "I'm depressed because they didn't want me," "If they gave me the job, I would be happy."*

The emotions you feel are in you, not in the outer world. No one can cause you to feel or emote in a particular way; if they're able to, it's only because you let them. A great way to let a harmful emotion pass is to observe it; and a good start is by giving it a name and seeing it as powerless.

It's commonplace to blame others for our pain. Instead of seeing the emotion for what it is and letting it pass, we've been taught to rely on dependencies, like asshole behavior, to manage the emotional reaction. Wake up! Emotions are not you.

*10 minutes of silence and focused breathing. Repeat the mantra: *"I am not an emotion. Emotions always pass."*

Day 16
(Share this experience using #30DaysSilentSong)

Exercise:

Choose a song to listen to carefully. You can choose the song from your music collection; or simply turn on the radio and wait for a song to play.

While listening to the song, don't listen to the notes, beats, voice, or rhythm; instead, listen for the silence between sounds. Listen for the stops, pauses, and absence of sound between notes. Listen for the silence in the song.

Have you ever realized that your favorite songs would not exist without silence? Every note, rhythm, beat, and voice needs a moment of silence to manifest – even if that moment exists in a millisecond. Without silence, there would be no noise, yet alone music. This isn't to say that noise and silence are in conflict; quite the opposite actually. Sounds and silence are complementary. So, were you able to hear the silence within the song? Practice this repeatedly whenever you listen to music. Listen for the silence that allows the music to endure.

Similarly, we need silence in order to let the rhythm of life manifest. Unfortunately, this has become a struggle for many people, because we live in an unbalanced world that encourages sound over silence. Don't follow noise dependent crowds, and don't fear silence. Silence is a powerful remedy. Practice remaining in silence daily; you'll start to hear and see new and wonderful things.

*15 minutes of silence and focused breathing. Repeat the mantra: **"Be silent. Listen. Be silent."**

Day 17
(Share this experience using #30DaysHobby)

Exercise:

On a sheet of paper (one that you can easily save and return to later) make a list of hobbies that you've had in the past but have neglected, and also make a list of hobbies that you would like to start in the future.

From these lists choose one hobby from the past and one new hobby that you'd like to start. Focus only on these two – the old hobby and the new one. Make this a priority.

How often have you said, or have heard other people say, *"I wish I had the time."* You do have the time. You just choose to think of time in the way that you've been taught to perceive it. If your life depended on it, you would certainly make the time if needed.

In fact, time is a manmade construct - don't ever forget that. There is only the present moment. Past and future are not here and now. We spend far too much time thinking about time. How many of your recurrent inner thoughts involve questions such as, *"When will that ever happen?" "When will I ever change?" "Why did that have to happen?" "If the past were different, life would be better."* These are lies that only eat into the present moment, and infect our modern world.

Asshole habits, patterns of thinking, and behavior occupy the present moment; and that moment could be used to pursue hobbies that magnify your happiness.

*15 minutes of silence and focused breathing. Repeat the mantra: *"**The time is now. Happiness is present.**"*

Day 18
(Share this experience using #30DaysCoffin)

Exercise:

Lay down on the floor (not on a bed or couch), with your back straight and your arms at your side. Close your eyes.

Now, imagine yourself in a coffin or under the ground. If this depresses you, do it regardless. With your eyes closed, imagine not being able to open them ever again; also imagine not being able to move your body or speaking ever again. Stay in this position for 10 minutes, or as long as you can.

If this seems gothic or dark, that's only your learned perception of the death experience. There's an ancient teaching that says the way to enlightenment is through a keen awareness of death. The person who is daily reminded that the body will die, and faces this fact head on with a clear mind and acceptance, has nothing to lose and is truly free to live in the present moment. The question isn't whether or not your body will die (because it surely will); the more important question is will you live before death?

Will you truly live before your body dies? The present moment is the only thing you'll always experience. Instead of fearing a pending death, accept it and be thankful for the present moment, and live in it! Don't spend the present moment being an asshole any longer.

*15 minutes of silence and focused breathing. Repeat the mantra: **"My body will age and pass, but I will always be present."**

Day 19
(Share this experience using #30DaysDress)

Exercise:

This exercise will require a bit of courage. If you believe it'll cause too much anxiety, then there will be an alternative below. Assuming it's warmer weather, put on a shirt backward and go to a public place (store, park, movie theater, walk around the block, etc). If it's colder weather, go to a public place wearing your hat inside out, two different shoes or boots, or a jacket inside out. In other words, go into a public place dressed in a piece of clothing that is worn oddly or wrong.

If you can't, or won't, do this; then wear a shirt backwards around your home until you go to bed.

What thoughts and feelings did you experience during this exercise? Did your behavior change in any way, or your interaction with people? Did changing the way you wore clothing change you? People put a lot of worry, concern, and thought into what they wear. Judgments abound in certain societies that consider clothing a necessity for identity; and just like many societal customs, clothing trends and styles change.

If you identify with your clothing, you'll remain unaware of yourself in the present moment. Wear clothes, but don't let clothing cover your true being; experience the present moment without the hindrance of apparel, fashion, or style.

*15 minutes of silence and focused breathing. Repeat the mantra: **"I am not a style or brand. I am a free being."**

Day 20
(Share this experience using #30DaysCount)

Exercise:

Count to 25 slowly, pausing for a few seconds before the next number; then, count backward from 25 slowly. Try this with your eyes closed. While counting up you can imagine yourself being lifted into the sky; and then while counting down, descending back to earth.

Our world today is about speed. Everyone seems to be in a rush, yet most of people are unsatisfied; and, they have no clue where they're going. Chasing the next best thing is a fruitless endeavor. It's the rare person who slows down to enjoy the present moment, regardless of its nature. Because there seems to be so many problems, and most jobs are focused on resolving those problems, people are compelled to accept anxiety and rush toward a reward and conclusion. That surely isn't happiness. Happiness can only be found in the present moment, not in a hypothetical future of rewards and successes. Rushing is another form of going nowhere.

How many times have you rushed through the day as an asshole? This is destructive to your peace of mind and health: concentration suffers, stress levels rise, and awareness to the present moment isn't possible.

It's critical to slow down. You only have one life to live – don't rush through it, and don't be dependent on anything that encourages you to rush. Be still, and slow down.

*15 minutes of silence and focused breathing. Repeat the mantra: *"Slow down. Do not rush. Enjoy the present moment."*

Day 21

(Share this experience using #30DaysSymbol)

Exercise:

Choose a physical symbol that will remind you to observe and be aware in the present moment. Try to choose something from nature, or that is made of natural material.

The object you choose can be anything, but it's best if it's something that you can enjoy looking at and touching. For example, many walkers and hikers will find a unique rock small enough to carry in their hands. A stone, necklace, bracelet, seashell, cedar block, coin…anything will do, as long as you enjoy it and you can dedicate it as a tool for remembrance.

Another cunning trick of asshole behavior is to confuse the mind into forgetting you're part of the natural world. Asshole tendencies require you to use the imagination, which can be easily manipulated for the business of being an asshole. Thus, you're taken out of physical reality. By having a symbol of remembrance, you can reconnect with the present moment. This symbol isn't meant to be an idol, god, or icon. Don't think too deeply into this. The symbol is simply a tool to help you remember where you are in the *here and now*. As long as you're aware of the present, you'll have no desire to return to the hallucination of being an asshole.

*15 minutes of silence and focused breathing. Repeat the mantra: *"All is well. Here and now, all is well."*

Day 22
(Share this experience using #30DaysSmile)

Exercise:

Hold a smile for 5 minutes. You don't need to do this exercise in front of a mirror; but feel free to do so if you wish. You can even do this exercise during the 15 minutes of silence and focused breathing. While holding your smile, take a moment and feel your face; actually touch the smile and the curvature of your lips and cheek bones.

Have you ever behaved a certain way and then saw your mood change immediately? Physical exercise, such as running and weightlifting, does this for many people. Certain forms of yoga have also been used by people to change their moods. The point is: changing your behavior not only impacts other people, but can also impact your perception of yourself.

You'll notice that while you're smiling during this exercise, you may experience certain emotions. You might feel silly, embarrassed, weird, or stupid. Continue smiling regardless. In fact, if you are still being an asshole at this point in the program, smile while you're in asshole mode – hold the smile until you are through with the asshole experience; set a reminder alarm if needed. As always, observe your thoughts while you're smiling; observe the thoughts as if they're clouds passing by in a bright blue sky.

Smiling causes an authentic reaction in our bodies and minds that is essentially good. The present moment enjoys a nice smile. So hold that smile until you no longer can.

*15 minutes of silence and focused breathing. Repeat the mantra: *"Happiness is now. I am happy."*

Day 23

(Share this experience using #30DaysFocus)

Exercise:

Focus on a natural object or scene for 10 minutes, without distraction and in silence.

Focusing on a natural object for an extended period of time is an ancient practice. How often have you stopped to observe something objectively for more than 10 minutes? When was the last time you've quietly watched a sunset, sunrise, tree sway in the wind, bird chirping, clouds passing or expanding, or just a rock? That might sound boring, but this practice is very liberating. If you look at anything long enough you start to see it from a different perspective. As easy as this exercise sounds, it's not – try it out, and see how long you can observe without thoughts impeding the practice.

Watching a bird feed may be more interesting than watching an immobile rock; but I encourage you to start with an immobile object, such as a stone or piece of wood. During this process thoughts will emerge – observe the thoughts and let them pass. Don't attach a goal or benchmark of success to this exercise; just observe an object.

Asshole behavior wants to hypnotize you with a false narrative; stealing your attention from the present moment.

*15 minutes of silence and focused breathing. Repeat the mantra: *"Be focused. Observe. Be present."*

Day 24
(Share this experience using #30DaysPinch)

Exercise:

Pinch the skin on the back of your hand or forearm until there is discomfort and slight pain. It's not necessary to pinch hard enough to bruise yourself, just enough to feel a small burn.

Did I cause the pain by asking you to do this exercise? No; you caused this pain to yourself – think about this carefully. You even decided how much pain to give yourself, and when to relieve the pain. You can't blame me or anyone else for the pain you just experienced. You were solely responsible. You were also responsible for letting go.

This is easily understood with regard to physical pain, such as pinching oneself; however, we have a lot of difficulty understanding this lesson as it applies to adverse emotions and feelings. How often have you said, and have heard others say, *"He makes me so angry when..."*, *"I'm depressed because she..."*, or *"I'm so frustrated that they..."* No person ever makes you experience negative feelings. It's always you who are experiencing them; and then placing the blame on others. Essentially, you are emotionally pinching yourself and not letting go. People go their entire lives without releasing the pinch. Instead of letting go, they scream at others, *"Release the pain! Let go! Fix this! Stop this! You're to blame!"* Wake up and see that you are solely responsible for letting go of the pain, and you can do it now.

*15 minutes of silence and focused breathing. Repeat the mantra: **"I can release negative feelings, here and now."**

Day 25

(Share this experience using #30DaysSway)

Exercise:

Stand still for 5 minutes; with knees slightly bent (i.e. your legs should not be locked). At first try to remain still, but then let your body sway. Let it move any way it wishes. Feel its movement. If you're unable to stand, you can do this same exercise by extending your arm or leg from a sitting position – try to keep it straight, but then let go of trying and allow movement to happen.

We tend to lock ourselves into particular goals, expectations, thought patterns, and habits. We even go so far as to admire and honor rigidity – people mistake rigidity for perseverance. This is taught and told to us by our culture. Everything around you may be shouting, even in a quiet whisper, that you must remain submissive and obedient.

Asshole behavior, like most dependencies, is no different in its message. It wants you to remain rigid; not to be released from its hold. If you freely moved on from being an asshole, it would lose you as a dependent. By the way, who wants to remain rigidly dependent on something like being an asshole for their false happiness?

The message of asshole behavior essentially says, *"It's OK being an asshole. You'll always be an asshole. This is your true self. Be proud to be an asshole."* Allow your body and mind to move on from being an asshole. Trust that your body and mind will sway to its own rhythm.

*15 minutes of silence and focused breathing. Repeat the mantra: *"I am now free to move. I am free to move on."*

Day 26
(Share this experience using #30DaysWalk)

Exercise:

Go for a mindfulness walk for at least 10 minutes. Focus on each step. Feel the steps: the feel of your feet hitting the ground, your heel rolling forward, your toes, the bend of your knees, your hips working to balance your posture, the swinging of your arms, etc. Don't rush; go slow. Focus on your breathing as well. Get in tune with your body. Pay attention to your physical senses throughout the walk. Focus – don't listen to music or be distracted.

Human beings have always used walking as a naturally restorative exercise. There is something about walking, and focusing on the walk, that calms the mind and soul. The longer one walks, the more relaxed one feels.

Any moment is a good time to walk and experience your inner and outer environment. During long walks, thoughts will emerge that will allow you to consciously observe them. Let the thoughts pass; you may even have emotions that emerge, observe those and let them pass as well. Focusing on your steps will help you clear the mind of clutter. Walking in the early morning and at dusk is especially beneficial.

A 20 minute walk brings more comfort, stillness, peace, focus, and awareness than thousands of hours of being an asshole. Walk every day, as much as you can.

*15 minutes of silence and focused breathing. Repeat the mantra: "**I am relaxed. I am at peace.**"

Day 27

(Share this experience using #30DaysLies)

Exercise:

On a sheet of paper (any size) write down all the internal lies that you regularly hear about yourself – i.e. within your mind.

Now, tear the paper into multiple pieces, and throw away.

It's common to have an internal voice (or voices) within your mind, playing a record of lies over and over. We eventually begin to accept these lies and let them impact our growth and happiness. Most people you see on a daily basis have these recurring internal voices; and most people are oblivious to them – sort of like white noise. This isn't a mental illness, but a way in which the mind works. We all experience these internal quiet voices whispering untruths about our being. These lies are nothing to fear, but they need to be observed. Writing them down can help you observe and become aware of their deceptions.

The power of silence, focused breathing, and mantras, which you have been practicing, is to draw out the lies. Let them manifest, and observe them. Common internal lies include: *"You are a loser," "You have become nothing, and you will never improve," "You are worthless. No one likes you," "You'll always be alone," "You're a burden,"* and so on. These thoughts are not part of you; however, the deception is to make you believe they are. Like many things in our culture, asshole patterns of thinking and behavior implants many of these lies clandestinely.

*15 minutes of silence and focused breathing. Repeat the mantra: "**Thoughts are only thoughts - nothing more.**"

Day 28
(Share this experience using #30DaysDoorway)

Exercise:

Stand in front of a doorway, with the door open. Close your eyes, and take a deep breath. With eyes closed and holding your breath, step through the doorway. Once you have stepped through completely, open your eyes and exhale.

Doorways are amazing tools that can be used for practicing mindfulness and observation. How often do you rush through doors without paying attention to the change of environment? We don't often pay attention or appreciate the transition; we simply rush through unaware that our perspective has changed. This isn't a bad thing; in fact, it's great that we don't stall in front of doorways, too afraid to enter the next environment. At the beginning of this exercise you were in a particular place, and then you stepped through a doorway into a completely different setting. You made a transition without worry or concern, and very naturally.

When it comes to physical doorways, we rarely stop and worry about the change of environment – we just walk through and accept the new experience. You can apply this same lesson to decisions that have you stressed, anxious, or worried. Step through the decision and accept the change; but try to step through aware and grateful. There will always be a doorway leading to new experiences.

*15 minutes of silence and focused breathing. Repeat the mantra: *"I accept change with awareness and gratitude."*

Day 29

(Share this experience using #30DaysLaugh)

Exercise:

Make yourself laugh for 5 minutes. Don't stop laughing. You might feel strange, weird, embarrassed, or stupid...it doesn't matter, just laugh. Try to laugh alone and without the aid of a comedy or joke. If you don't know how to start, just start making the noises that typically accompany your laughter.

What feelings did you experience during this exercise? Many people report feeling embarrassed or goofy, which is great; however, most people also report a feeling of relief and buoyancy when they've completed this exercise.

Similar to holding a smile, laughing for 5 minutes is a fantastic way to come into present awareness. If you think about it, humor is necessary for life. How sad is the person who is unable to laugh at the experiences of life? After all, life is funny, even the dreadful and lousy experiences.

If you ever again experience adverse thoughts and feelings that accompany being an asshole, simply laugh at them. Consider how crazy and frivolous it is to be an asshole; it really is a funny dependency. No other living thing on the planet becomes dependent on being an asshole. The entire situation is comical. If you perceive asshole thoughts and behaviors for what they truly are - fictitious, impractical, and frivolous dependencies – then they can be easily dropped. You must learn to laugh. Genuinely laugh the asshole away.

*15 minutes of silence and focused breathing. Repeat the mantra: **"Life is wonderful, funny, and real."**

Day 30
(Share this experience using #30DaysThanks)

Exercise:

Take a piece of paper (one that you can keep) and write down all that you are grateful for – these things don't have to be in any particular order of importance.

Next to each thing you list, write "Thank you."

The person who isn't thankful for all that life gives is typically quite miserable; and assholes thrive on that misery. The truly grateful person can let go of anything at anytime. A thankful person is always a happy person, so practice gratitude daily.

Have you ever heard anyone say, "*I'm so grateful for being an asshole*"? Nobody is thankful for being an asshole; which is a clear sign that it's a destructive dependency. However, a few people have learned to be thankful for the present moment experience.

Not only is it unhealthy, but the dependency on being an asshole discourages a grateful mind and soul. With only one life to live in the present moment, it's important to always emphasize a grateful heart. Spend time with people who are grateful, and do things that nourish a thankful heart in the present moment. Anything that encourages misery and depression isn't worth giving attention to. Be thankful, always.

*15 minutes of silence and focused breathing. Repeat the mantra: "**I am grateful. I am thankful.**"

Conclusion

The exercises and lessons in this program taught and encouraged observation, awareness to your present moment experience, change of perception, and awakening to true happiness, which can only be found right now at this moment. You were shown that your negative thoughts and feelings are not caused by being an asshole, or any unhealthy reliance, but are solely within you and illusory; which means that you are capable of letting those asshole thoughts and feelings pass and dropping the illusion of being an asshole.

As mentioned at the beginning, there were no goals or measures of success for this program. If you were hoping to find a reason to stop or continue being an asshole, then you may be spending too much time struggling and thinking about being an asshole. This was not meant to be a struggle, but a release.

Life is not meant to be spent being an asshole, or relying on any type of toxic behavior or pattern of thinking. Wake up to the present moment and enjoy your present experience. If you've made it through the program, you are certainly more awakened then when you started; however, don't give up mindfully practicing observation of thoughts and feelings, stillness, silence, deep and focused breathing, allowing everything to pass, laughing, smiling, and being grateful.

Live wonderfully awakened and aware…with or without being an asshole.

Notes for Day 1

(Use this page to write down thoughts, reminders, ideas, prayers, mantras, revelations, lessons, modifications to the exercise, or experiences. If you'd like to share something, please post using **#30DaysNow** or use the exercise's unique hashtag.)

Notes for Day 2
(Use this page to write down thoughts, reminders, ideas, prayers, mantras, revelations, lessons, modifications to the exercise, or experiences. If you'd like to share something, please post using #30DaysNow or use the exercise's unique hashtag.)

Notes for Day 3

(Use this page to write down thoughts, reminders, ideas, prayers, mantras, revelations, lessons, modifications to the exercise, or experiences. If you'd like to share something, please post using **#30DaysNow** or use the exercise's unique hashtag.)

Notes for Day 4
(Use this page to write down thoughts, reminders, ideas, prayers, mantras, revelations, lessons, modifications to the exercise, or experiences. If you'd like to share something, please post using **#30DaysNow** or use the exercise's unique hashtag.)

Notes for Day 5

(Use this page to write down thoughts, reminders, ideas, prayers, mantras, revelations, lessons, modifications to the exercise, or experiences. If you'd like to share something, please post using **#30DaysNow** or use the exercise's unique hashtag.)

Notes for Day 6

(Use this page to write down thoughts, reminders, ideas, prayers, mantras, revelations, lessons, modifications to the exercise, or experiences. If you'd like to share something, please post using **#30DaysNow** or use the exercise's unique hashtag.)

(50)

Notes for Day 7

(Use this page to write down thoughts, reminders, ideas, prayers, mantras, revelations, lessons, modifications to the exercise, or experiences. If you'd like to share something, please post using **#30DaysNow** or use the exercise's unique hashtag.)

Notes for Day 8

(Use this page to write down thoughts, reminders, ideas, prayers, mantras, revelations, lessons, modifications to the exercise, or experiences. If you'd like to share something, please post using **#30DaysNow** or use the exercise's unique hashtag.)

Notes for Day 9

(Use this page to write down thoughts, reminders, ideas, prayers, mantras, revelations, lessons, modifications to the exercise, or experiences. If you'd like to share something, please post using **#30DaysNow** or use the exercise's unique hashtag.)

Notes for Day 10

(Use this page to write down thoughts, reminders, ideas, prayers, mantras, revelations, lessons, modifications to the exercise, or experiences. If you'd like to share something, please post using **#30DaysNow** or use the exercise's unique hashtag.)

Notes for Day 11

(Use this page to write down thoughts, reminders, ideas, prayers, mantras, revelations, lessons, modifications to the exercise, or experiences. If you'd like to share something, please post using **#30DaysNow** or use the exercise's unique hashtag.)

Notes for Day 12

(Use this page to write down thoughts, reminders, ideas, prayers, mantras, revelations, lessons, modifications to the exercise, or experiences. If you'd like to share something, please post using **#30DaysNow** or use the exercise's unique hashtag.)

Notes for Day 13

(Use this page to write down thoughts, reminders, ideas, prayers, mantras, revelations, lessons, modifications to the exercise, or experiences. If you'd like to share something, please post using **#30DaysNow** or use the exercise's unique hashtag.)

Notes for Day 14

(Use this page to write down thoughts, reminders, ideas, prayers, mantras, revelations, lessons, modifications to the exercise, or experiences. If you'd like to share something, please post using **#30DaysNow** or use the exercise's unique hashtag.)

Notes for Day 15

(Use this page to write down thoughts, reminders, ideas, prayers, mantras, revelations, lessons, modifications to the exercise, or experiences. If you'd like to share something, please post using **#30DaysNow** or use the exercise's unique hashtag.)

Notes for Day 16

(Use this page to write down thoughts, reminders, ideas, prayers, mantras, revelations, lessons, modifications to the exercise, or experiences. If you'd like to share something, please post using **#30DaysNow** or use the exercise's unique hashtag.)

Notes for Day 17

(Use this page to write down thoughts, reminders, ideas, prayers, mantras, revelations, lessons, modifications to the exercise, or experiences. If you'd like to share something, please post using **#30DaysNow** or use the exercise's unique hashtag.)

Notes for Day 18
(Use this page to write down thoughts, reminders, ideas, prayers, mantras, revelations, lessons, modifications to the exercise, or experiences. If you'd like to share something, please post using **#30DaysNow** or use the exercise's unique hashtag.)

Notes for Day 19

(Use this page to write down thoughts, reminders, ideas, prayers, mantras, revelations, lessons, modifications to the exercise, or experiences. If you'd like to share something, please post using **#30DaysNow** or use the exercise's unique hashtag.)

Notes for Day 20

(Use this page to write down thoughts, reminders, ideas, prayers, mantras, revelations, lessons, modifications to the exercise, or experiences. If you'd like to share something, please post using **#30DaysNow** or use the exercise's unique hashtag.)

Notes for Day 21

(Use this page to write down thoughts, reminders, ideas, prayers, mantras, revelations, lessons, modifications to the exercise, or experiences. If you'd like to share something, please post using **#30DaysNow** or use the exercise's unique hashtag.)

Notes for Day 22

(Use this page to write down thoughts, reminders, ideas, prayers, mantras, revelations, lessons, modifications to the exercise, or experiences. If you'd like to share something, please post using **#30DaysNow** or use the exercise's unique hashtag.)

Notes for Day 23

(Use this page to write down thoughts, reminders, ideas, prayers, mantras, revelations, lessons, modifications to the exercise, or experiences. If you'd like to share something, please post using **#30DaysNow** or use the exercise's unique hashtag.)

Notes for Day 24

(Use this page to write down thoughts, reminders, ideas, prayers, mantras, revelations, lessons, modifications to the exercise, or experiences. If you'd like to share something, please post using **#30DaysNow** or use the exercise's unique hashtag.)

Notes for Day 25

(Use this page to write down thoughts, reminders, ideas, prayers, mantras, revelations, lessons, modifications to the exercise, or experiences. If you'd like to share something, please post using #30DaysNow or use the exercise's unique hashtag.)

Notes for Day 26

(Use this page to write down thoughts, reminders, ideas, prayers, mantras, revelations, lessons, modifications to the exercise, or experiences. If you'd like to share online, please post using **#30DaysNow** or use the exercise's unique hashtag.)

Notes for Day 27

(Use this page to write down thoughts, reminders, ideas, prayers, mantras, revelations, lessons, modifications to the exercise, or experiences. If you'd like to share something, please post using **#30DaysNow** or use the exercise's unique hashtag.)

Notes for Day 28

(Use this page to write down thoughts, reminders, ideas, prayers, mantras, revelations, lessons, modifications to the exercise, or experiences. If you'd like to share something, please post using **#30DaysNow** or use the exercise's unique hashtag.)

Notes for Day 29
(Use this page to write down thoughts, reminders, ideas, prayers, mantras, revelations, lessons, modifications to the exercise, or experiences. If you'd like to share something, please post using #30DaysNow or use the exercise's unique hashtag.)

Notes for Day 30

(Use this page to write down thoughts, reminders, ideas, prayers, mantras, revelations, lessons, modifications to the exercise, or experiences. If you'd like to share something, please post using **#30DaysNow** or use the exercise's unique hashtag.)

To be mindful is to experience life in the present moment...it's the only moment we have.

Don't forget to leave an online review.

Thank you!

Printed in Great Britain
by Amazon